OFF ROAD VEHICLES

JEEP WRANGLERS

KENNY ABDO

abdopublishing.com

Published by Abdo Zoom, a division of ABDO, PO Box 398166, Minneapolis, Minnesota 55439. Copyright © 2018 by Abdo Consulting Group, Inc. International copyrights reserved in all countries. No part of this book may be reproduced in any form without written permission from the publisher. Bolt!™ is a trademark and logo of Abdo Zoom.

Printed in the United States of America, North Mankato, Minnesota.
092017
012018

Photo Credits: Alamy, AP Images, Getty Images, iStock, Shutterstock
Production Contributors: Kenny Abdo, Jennie Forsberg, Grace Hansen
Design Contributors: Dorothy Toth, Neil Klinepier

Publisher's Cataloging-in-Publication Data

Names: Abdo, Kenny, author.
Title: Jeep Wranglers / by Kenny Abdo.
Description: Minneapolis, Minnesota: Abdo Zoom, 2018. | Series: Off road vehicles |
    Includes online resource and index.
Identifiers: LCCN 2017939274 | ISBN 9781532121029 (lib.bdg.) |
    ISBN 9781532122149 (ebook) | ISBN 9781532122705 (Read-to-Me ebook)
Subjects: LCSH: Jeep Wrangler--Juvenile literature. | Vehicles--Juvenile literature. |
    Motor Sports—Juvenile literature.
Classification: DDC 629.2222--dc23
LC record available at https://lccn.loc.gov/2017939274

TABLE OF CONTENTS

JEEP
WRANGLER

The Jeep Wrangler is a four-wheel drive off-road vehicle. It is popular for its ability to travel on many types of terrain.

It can drive on sandy beaches and through deserts. It can even handle snow!

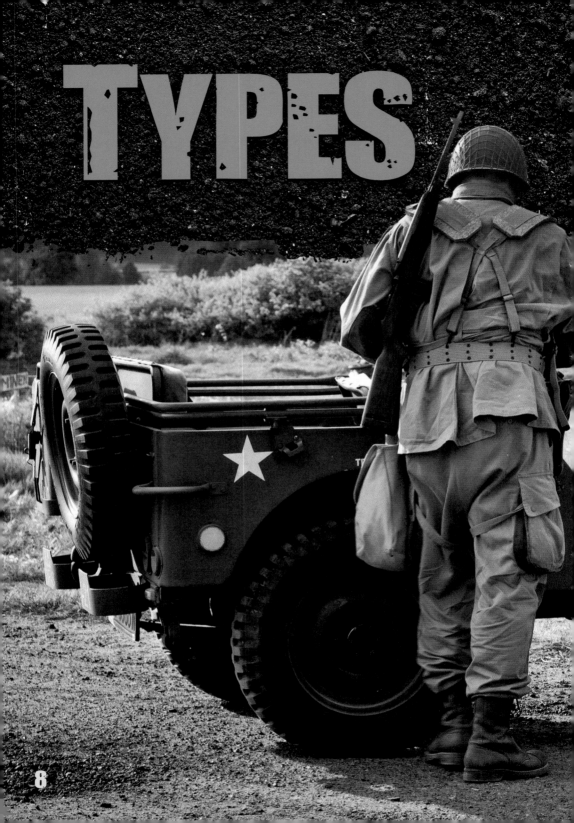

TYPES

The first Jeep was created during World War II. It was called the Willys MB. It was used to move U.S. Army soldiers quickly.

U.S.A.
M 547342

TP 25

FROM U.S. PORT AGENCY
WAR SHIPPING ADM. N.Y.

ROAD WT   2315 LBS.
GROSS WT   3125 LBS.
LENGTH   132 IN.
WIDTH   62 IN.
HEIGHT   52 IN.

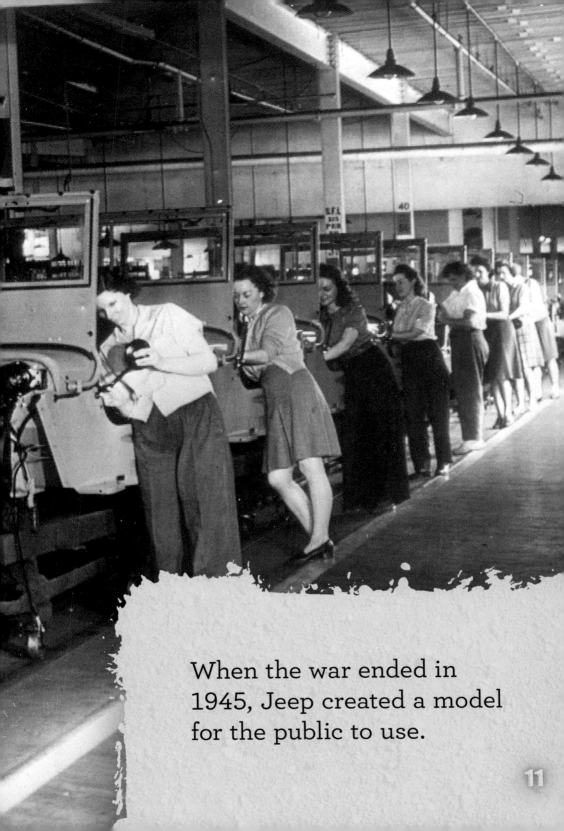

When the war ended in 1945, Jeep created a model for the public to use.

The vehicle was called the CJ model, which is short for Civilian Jeep. It was used for construction, farming, and deliveries.

The Jeep CJ was renamed the Jeep Wrangler in 1987.

"Jeeping" is a an activity
that some Jeep owners
like to do.

In 1953, the first **Jeep Jamboree** was held on the **Rubicon Trail.** The **trek** was 22 miles (35 km) long.

Now, Jeep Jamborees happen every year. The Expediciones De Las Americas was a 21,000-mile (33,796 km) trip. Drivers moved over the roughest terrain from Chile to Alaska.

GLOSSARY

Jeep Jamboree – off-road adventures where Jeep owners ride together.

off-road – riding a vehicle on difficult roads or tracks, like sand, mud or gravel.

Rubicon Trail – part 4x4 trail and part road path, located in the Sierra Nevada.

terrain – a piece of land having certain features.

trek – a long, hard trip.

World War II – (1939 to 1945) a war fought in Europe, Asia, and Africa. Great Britain, France, the United States, the Soviet Union, and their allies were on one side. Germany, Italy, Japan, and their allies were on the other side.

ONLINE RESOURCES

Booklinks
NONFICTION NETWORK
FREE! ONLINE NONFICTION RESOURCES

To learn more about Jeep Wranglers, please visit abdobooklinks.com. These links are routinely monitored and updated to provide the most current information available.

INDEX